Magnets

Karen Bryant-Mole

Heinemann Interactive Library
Des Plaines, Illinois

First published in the United States by Heinemann Interactive Library,
an imprint of Reed Educational & Professional Publishing,
1350 East Touhy Avenue, Suite 240 West
Des Plaines, IL 60018

Printed in Hong Kong / China
Designed by Jean Wheeler
Commissioned photography by Zul Mukhida
Consultant—Hazel Grice

© BryantMole Books 1998

02 01 00 99
10 9 8 7 6 5 4 3 2

Library of Congress Cataloging-in-Publication Data
Bryant-Mole, Karen.
    Magnets / by Karen Bryant-Mole.
        p.   cm. -- (Science all around me)
    Includes bibliographical references and index.
    Summary: Text and experiments introduce the scientific properties
  of magnets, examining such topics as their strength, magnetic poles,
  and the making of magnets.
    ISBN 1-57572-629-7 (library binding)
    1. Magnets--Juvenile literature. 2. Magnets--Experiments-
-Juvenile literature. [1. Magnets. 2. Magnets--Experiments.
3. Magnetism. 4. Magnetism--Experiments. 5. Experiments.]
I. Title. II. Series.
QC757.5.B79   1998
538'.4--dc21   97-41943
                                                             CIP
                                                              AC

A number of questions are posed in this book. They are designed
to consolidate children's understanding by encouraging further
exploration of the science in their everyday lives.

Acknowledgements
The Publishers would like to thank the following for permission to reproduce photographs: Positive Images p. 6,
Zefa pp. 4, 10, 14.

Every effort had been made to contact copyright holders of any material reproduced in this book. Any omissions will be
rectified in subsequent printings if notice is given to the Publisher.

Words that appear in the text in bold can be found in the glossary.

Contents

Magnets

There is a huge magnet hanging from this crane.

A magnet is a metal that some other metals **cling** to.

Large pieces of squashed metal are clinging to this magnet.

(i) *Things that can cling to a magnet are called "magnetic."*

See for yourself...

Billy cut out some
fish shapes. Then he put a
paperclip on each fish and
placed them in a pretend
pond.

He made a fishing rod from
a stick, some string, and a
magnet. The paperclips
on the fish cling to the
magnet.

Billy can pull the
fish out of the pond.

Magnetic or Non-magnetic?

Iron is a magnetic metal. It will **cling** to a magnet. Other metals that have iron in them, such as steel, are also magnetic.

This boy is putting a metal can into a **recycling** bin. Magnets will be used to sort the cans with iron in them from those without iron.

? *Does your family recycle cans?*

See for yourself...

Melissa is testing some objects with a magnet.

Magnets that are this shape are called bar magnets.

Things that won't cling to a magnet are "non-magnetic." This plastic spoon is non-magnetic.

Magnetic Force

These keys are **clinging** to two long, thin magnets. They are being pulled to the magnets by a force called magnetism.

A force is a **scientific** word for a type of push or pull.

(i) *When something is pulled toward a magnet, it is "attracted" by the magnet.*

See for yourself...

Billy and Alice are playing a travel game.

The board is magnetic. The playing pieces have tiny magnets attached to them.

Billy can feel the magnetic pull when he tries to move a playing piece.

Magnetism through Air

Magnets work through air.

This freezer door has a magnetic strip down the side of the door.

When the woman shuts the door, she will feel the magnetism pulling, even when there is still a gap between the freezer and the door.

? *Can you think of any doors in your home that might have magnetic strips?*

10

See for yourself...

Carl is lowering a magnet over some paperclips.

Magnets that are this shape are called horseshoe magnets.

Just before the magnet reaches the paperclips, he sees that they jump up to **cling** to the magnet.

The magnetic force has pulled them up through the air.

Magnetism through Objects

Behind each of these little wooden butterflies is a magnet.

The magnets are **clinging** to a magnetic refrigerator door.

Between the magnets and the door there are pieces of paper.

ⓘ *Magnetism can work through non-magnetic materials like paper.*

See for yourself...

Adam used some refrigerator magnets and a magnetic **baking pan** to see if the magnet worked through other non-magnetic materials.

He found that the thickness of the material was important.

The magnets worked through thin pieces of plastic, cardboard, and **fabric** but not thicker pieces.

Strength

Some magnets are stronger than others.

Refrigerator magnets are quite weak but this magnet is very strong. It can be used to lift lots of metal.

ⓘ *Magnets pull on magnetic materials. The stronger the magnet, the greater its pull.*

See for yourself...

Alex has two magnets.

She put two paperclips on the edge of a table and slowly pushed one magnet towards one of the paperclips until it started to move.

The second magnet has been pushed in much closer but the second paperclip has still not moved.

The second magnet must be weaker.

Poles

This dressmaker is using a horseshoe magnet to pick up pins. The pins are **clinging** to the two ends.

The ends of a magnet are called its poles.

One end is called the north pole and the other the south pole.

(i) *The poles of a magnet have the strongest pull.*

16

See for yourself...

Kate has pushed a bar magnet into a pile of paperclips.

When she lifts the magnet, she can see that most of the paperclips are clinging to the ends of the magnet.

Two Magnets

These two magnets are **clinging** to each other.

If one magnet's north pole faces the other magnet's south pole, the two magnets will be attracted to each other.

If the same poles face each other, the magnets are pushed apart.

 Magnets pushing apart is called "repelling."

See for yourself...

Alice's toy train cars have a magnet on each end.

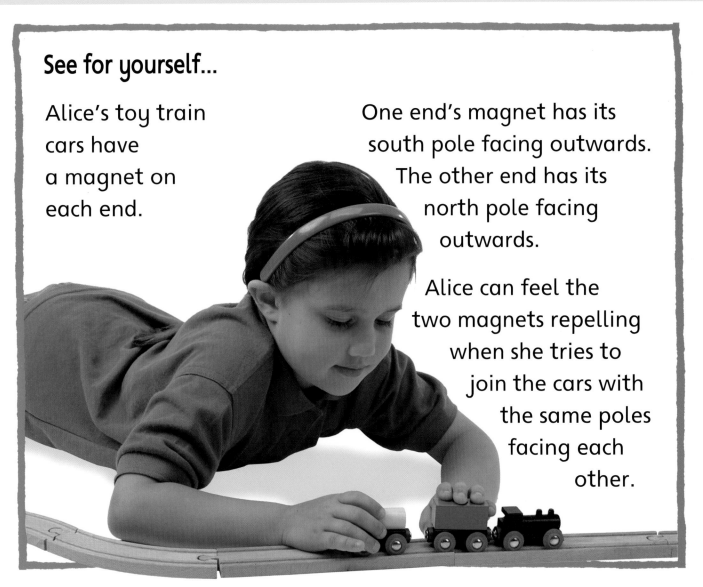

One end's magnet has its south pole facing outwards. The other end has its north pole facing outwards.

Alice can feel the two magnets repelling when she tries to join the cars with the same poles facing each other.

19

Making Magnets

When something that is made from a magnetic **material** touches a magnet, it too becomes a magnet.

Anything that becomes a magnet is called "magnetized." These paperclips are touching a magnet. They have become magnetized.

i *When the paperclips are taken off the magnet they stop being magnets.*

See for yourself...

Things that are only magnetized for a short time are called temporary magnets.

Adam has made a line of paperclips hang off this magnet.

Each new paperclip becomes magnetized and will attract the next paperclip.

When Adam takes them off the magnet, the paperclips stop being magnets.

Permanent Magnets

Anything that is a magnet all the time is called a permanent magnet.

These are all permanent magnets.

Magnets are made up of millions of tiny magnets, all facing the same direction.

ⓘ *If a magnet gets knocked, some of the tiny magnets may get moved and the magnet will lose some of its magnetism.*

See for yourself...

Permanent magnets slowly get weaker as time goes on.

Special pieces of soft iron, called "keepers," can help to stop this from happening.

Melissa is putting a keeper onto this horseshoe magnet.

The more care you take of your magnets, the longer they will last.

23

Glossary

attached fastened

baking pan a flat, metal tray

cling(-ing) is pulled in and held

fabric cloth

materials what things are made from

recycling using again

scientific to do with science

More Books to Read

Fowler, *What Magnets Can Do*. Danbury, CT: Children's Press. 1995.

Rowe, Julian & Perham, Molly. *Amazing Magnets*. Danbury, CT: Children's Press. 1994.

Ward, Alan. *Magnets & Electricity*. Danbury, CT: Franklin Watts. 1992.

Index